MW00958969

"Stay Real!

Foreword by Brian Francis Hume

Bill Yt

The Power of Real
Transparent Prophetic Encouragement

Inspiring Stories of Everyday Life

By Bill C. Yount

The Power of Real...Transparent Prophetic Encouragement
Copyright © 2017 by Bill C. Yount

Published by
Blowing the Shofar Ministries
132 E. North Ave.
Hagerstown, MD 21740
www.billyount.com

ISBN-13: 978-1975748975
ISBN-10: 1975748972

Printed in the United States of America
For Worldwide Distribution

Interior Layout & Design by Cheryl Jenkins
Cover Design by Bill Johnson

Table of Contents

Foreword: Brian Francis Hume 1
Acknowledgements 3
Introduction: Let's Be Honest - No More Cover Ups! 5

Section One - What Forty Years Have Taught Me

A. If It's Not Amazing, It's Not Grace 9
B. Sometimes Life Is Hard 11
C. You May Need the Person You Don't Like 12
D. Gnats the Size of Giants 13
E. A Dream in a Basket 15
F. Don't Die in Your Nest 16
G. Welcome to the Real World of Ministry 17
H. Don't Go Pickin' a Fight with the Devil 19
I. Giants Are the Breakfast of Champions 20
J. Take a Break! 22
K. God's Crazy Love Does It 23

Section Two - Being Real With You

A. Amazing Grace Is When You Think You Have
   Blown It 27
B. Do You Like How You Look? 29
C. Despite the Mud on My Face, I Have Struck Gold! 32
D. Did You Ever Get Mad at God? 37
E. Confessions of a Spirit-Led Writer 38
F. I Found the Secret to Healing in My Life 39
G. More Can Happen Over a Meal Than in Huge
   Conferences 40
H. Confessions of an Earthly Father 41

Section Three - God Is Going For the Real in Us

A. I Cried Out to God, "What Are You Doing To Me?" 44
B. A Titanic Move of God Is Coming Out of Deep,
   Troubled Waters 47

C. "I'm Using the Chaos In Your Life!" 50
D. "Don't Do It! " 52
E. This Is The Moment You Were Born For and
   The King Is Calling For You! 54
F. Stay Focused: Don't Compare Yourself To
   Anyone 59
G. The King Is Calling For Your Family 61
H. Talk About Freedom From Old Mindsets 63
I. I Want You to Do What You Don't Want to Do . . . 65
J. The Greatest Ear Specialist 66
K. Talk About Money 67
L. It's Time for The Harp, Pen, Paintbrush and
   Dancing Shoes 68
M. Prison Bars Are Melting 70
N. Rough Diamonds Are Getting God's Attention . . . 72
O. Stay Out of the Ring! 74
P. Many Are Coming In Out Of Left Field, Into My
   Kingdom 76

Section Four - Finding the Real in Others
A. Favored To Live 79
B. As Families Began Praying Together, I Heard
   the Heart of America Begin to Beat Again 83
C. Watch For Exit Signs to Light Up In This Season . 87
D. Are You a Trail Blazer? 91
E. Calling In Our Kingdom Reserves 93
F. An Earthly Father's Blessing 97
G. Be Patient, I'm Performing Major Heart Surgery
   On Your Nation 99
H. God Still Delivers 101

Section Five - Honest Nutrients

Major Victory - "I'm Uprooting Insecurity and Fear in My
                  People" 107
Dedication - Be Real and Be Healed! 110

Endorsements

"It has been an honor and joy to get to know Bill Yount in recent years. His gentle spirit and humorous disposition wrap his words around your heart like a warm blanket on a cold day. He is a true father in the faith with a heart for the generations. I highly recommend his writings as a way to be encouraged, strengthened, and renewed in your walk with the Lord."

Wanda Alger, Author of *"Oracles of Grace: Building a Legacy of Wisdom and Revelation" (2017).* www.wandaalger.me

"As one of today's most seasoned prophets, Bill Yount delivers a must-read message that encourages and stimulates us to grow in Christ. In his book, The Power of Real, Bill shares relevant accounts of how God used his soul-baring transparency and revelatory promptings from the Lord to speak to the body of Christ. You will be fed with fresh, extremely real, uplifting, prophetic rhema words. Bill vulnerably lays his life and ministry out on the table in a stripped bare, down-to-the-studs message within these pages. This is the book that Prophet Bill Yount will be remembered by."

Andy Sanders, Founder of www.capturingthesupernatural.com

"Absolutely fantastic! I love it! Bill nailed it!"

Linda Breitman - Author of *The Real You: Believing Your True Identity* - www.lindabreitman.com

"In the pages of this book: *The Power of Real*, Bill Yount beautifully and humbly illustrates through his own brokenness that the bumps, bruises and the pain of our past are not disqualifiers, but are that which qualifies us to better demonstrate the Father's love and grace to a heartbroken world."

Kevin Riordan - Evangelist - President of *Set Free Ministries* - www.setfreeweekends.com

Foreword

Since the late 90's, the reach of his pen mentored me through his prophetic writings posted on the Elijah List. His unique style was unlike anything else I'd read. Refreshingly honest. Oftentimes humorous. And always anointed.

After almost two decades, I finally met this man. His name? Bill Yount.

As I sat at the kitchen table, my anticipation was palpable. Here I was, sitting with a prophet I'd respected for years from afar. Since I did not know him other than through his writing, I was intrigued to learn more about him. What would he share with us? What would I learn about this prophet who travels all over the world?

Honestly, I wasn't prepared for what I was about to experience.

He was real. No pretense. Bill was void of self-flattery or any attempts to draw unnecessary attention to himself. As we broke bread around the table, he emptied himself. He shared stories. He asked questions. Altogether he was disarming. One question in particular stood out to me. The question was really an invitation.

With several ministers seated at the table, Bill shared how he struggled frequently when preparing to minister. *Huh?* I thought to myself, *Bill Yount struggles when preparing to minister?* I was a captive audience. He followed this statement with a question: *Do you also struggle when preparing to minister somewhere?*

Quietly, my heart screamed, *Yes, I struggle too with that!*

The question was an invitation to experience the Father's delight in me as a son, even in the midst of my struggles, weaknesses, and anxieties. It reminded me to be confident in His goodness so that I could be real and honest before Him - and transparent with others.

Are you ready for your invitation to experience God's transforming power of real?

Read *The Power of Real* with expectant faith that the Father's goodness will radically touch your heart. Bill Yount shares his very own life struggles. In doing so, it reveals the tenderness of the Father's heart that many have never encountered. You will read heartfelt stories from the author's own journey that will make you laugh, cry, and yearn to encounter Him. Bill's vulnerability unveiled through these pages is your invitation to embrace the Father's transforming power of real!

Brian Francis Hume
National Prayer Coordinator, *Awaken the Dawn*
Co-founder, *Breakthrough Tribe*
Intercessor, Revivalist, Writer
www.brianfrancishume.com

Acknowledgements

Thanks to my beautiful wife, Dagmar, for loving and praying for me to keep going. A special thank you to my son-in-law, for the long hours of editing. I didn't major in punctuation.

Thank you, Cheryl Jenkins, Founder of *Kingdom One Business Solutions*, for giving wisdom when needed.

I want to thank Linda Breitman for her inspiration and ideas for this book. Thank you, also, to Betsy Elliott, for helping to proof read it. I pray your new book, *A Journey of Love* will find its way into the hearts of children who read it.

Thank you, *Bridge of Life*, my home church, where I have attended for forty years as of now. You have been a pillar of love and support in my life and family all these years.

I am also honored to be a member of the *Apostolic Company of Alliance International Ministries*. Thank you for the priceless relationships we have built to advance God's kingdom.

I want to thank these prophetic websites for posting my writings: Spirit Fuel, Charisma Prophetic Insight and The Elijah List.

Most of all, thank you, Lord, for helping me write this fourth book. You always have something for me to write about.

"Transparency
SLAYS our giants.
That's the
power of being
real."

Introduction

Let's Be Honest, No More Cover Ups!

There seems to be a great gulf fixed between many pulpits and congregations and an even greater one between believers in Christ and the lost. The enemy has been very successful with convincing people that the pulpit is such a holy place that we can never measure up to the person behind it, or the Lord Himself. And the person who stands to minister hopes no one will ever know their weaknesses. It's a perfect lie from satan. Therefore, it can be tempting for pastors and churches to hide in fear of being real, not realizing the ground is all level at the foot of the cross. Ironically, why is it when you hear a pastor or leader even slightly mention that he has any kind of a problem, hope rises in the hearts of the listeners, encouraging us that we are not alone in our battles of life?

I believe it's high time for the body of Christ to be real about not only our victories, but also our struggles. If we are honest, for many of us, our struggles outweigh our victories. It's time we also become a safe place for the world to tell us where it hurts. This is where healing begins. Many who have read my writings say that what I write is transparent and down to earth. They see the treasure it carries comes through this earthen vessel.

I believe transparency shrinks our giants and the messages in this book will hopefully help do that in the lives of readers. Not only shrink them, but slay them. That's the power of being real.

This scripture was highlighted to me as I thought about what the Holy Spirit wants to convey through this book, *The Power of Real.*

Treasure in Clay Jars

"We are like common clay jars that carry this glorious treasure within, so that the extraordinary overflow of power will be seen as God's, not ours. Though we experience every kind of pressure, we're not crushed. At times we don't know what to do, but quitting is not an option. We are persecuted by others, but God has not forsaken us. We may be knocked down, but not out. We continually share in the death of Jesus in our own bodies so that the resurrection life of Jesus will be revealed through our humanity. We consider living to mean that we are constantly being handed over to death for Jesus' sake so that the life of Jesus will be revealed through our humanity. So, then, death is at work in us but it releases life in you."

2 Corinthians 4:7-12 (The Passion Translation Bible)

Section One

What Forty Years Have Taught Me

"Forty years
have taught
me how
much I
don't know."

If it's Not Amazing, It's Not Grace

I want to thank you Lord, for using the foolish, the weak, and the vulnerable, who never quite get it together, to bring glory to Your Name. You waste nothing. You are not surprised by our sins, failures, and the agony of defeat, but You are drawn closer to us through them. That's why You came and still come for us. It's difficult for me to wrap my mind around this fourth book. I wonder if I've been through enough fire in forty years that the fourth man, Jesus, may show up and show off in this one like never before. When I first came to You, I knew so much about everything. I had all the answers. Forty years have taught me how much I don't know, even about You. But this one thing I do know; "Jesus Christ and Him crucified" and I'm just beginning to realize how much He loves me. I now have the answer to every question: it's Jesus Christ, the Son of the Living God.

"He (the King) answered and said, Lo, I see four men loose, walking in the midst of the fire, and they have no hurt; and the form of the fourth is like the Son of God." Daniel 3:25 (KJV)

"I didn't count
on suffering
and I didn't
count
on pain."

Sometimes Life Is Hard

I never want to know anything about a church when I go to minister there. It can influence hearing what the Lord has to say. Years ago, the breaking news leaked out and reached me before I arrived at a certain church. The church was facing gigantic problems in the leadership and congregation. I was so overwhelmed with hearing about this that I felt I couldn't stand to minister in their pulpit. I said, "Lord, I don't know what to say to these people. I feel discouraged myself, hearing about their problems." I said, "Lord, what would You say to these people?" He said, "Tell them, 'SOMETIMES LIFE IS HARD!'"

I missed out on something when I first came to the Lord forty years ago. I didn't count on suffering and I didn't count on pain, but it came anyhow, sometimes like a river, other times like a flood. When trouble came, it hit me harder, for I didn't realize the promise, *"In the world ye shall have tribulation..."* John 16:33 (KJV)

I believe this is one of the reasons we live in an offended nation, an offended generation of believers and offended families. Lord, help us as followers of You to know that, although life is hard, we can be of good cheer, for You have overcome the world and with You inside us, we can too. Use us to heal the wounds and hurts of the nations.

"I have told you these things, so that in me you may have peace. In this world you will have trouble. But take heart! I have overcome the world." John 16:33 (NIV)

You May Need the Person You Don't Like

After walking with God and being in the same church for forty years, I have discovered something. God often puts something we need in the person we don't like. He seems to anoint people we wouldn't. The person who rubs you the wrong way may be the only one who has the gift of healing with the name of your sickness on it.

The person you are jealous of, could be the one who launches your ministry, if you humble yourself before them. The people who love you enough to confront you, are the ones you learn the most from. I once said, "Lord, are you trying to kill me with some crazy people around me?" He responded, "You're coming in to revelation now."

"It takes a grinding wheel to sharpen a blade, and so a friendly argument can sharpen a man." Proverbs 27:17 (The Passion Translation)

Gnats the Size of Giants

While washing my hands, a tiny gnat kept darting around my face. I swung to grab and kill it, but its miniscule size seemed to make it invincible as it swirled around my head, escaping my deadly hands. I thought to myself, "How can something so insignificant be tormenting me?"

I then heard the Lord speak, "Son, many times you feel small and insignificant in your own eyes, but you are a torment to the devil. That's why he swings so much at you, but you keep escaping. It's the devil that makes you feel insignificant, for when he sees you, he sees a gnat the size of a giant. Tell my people they are giants in the eyes of the enemy."

"Ye are of God, little children, and have overcome them: because greater is he that is in you, than he that is in the world." I John 4:4 (KJV)

"Is it

God's

dream or

yours?"

A Dream in a Basket

There comes a time when you must put your dream in a basket and lay it in the Nile River that's infested with alligators, snakes, and poisonous critters, and let it float downstream. Then you will know if it's God's dream for you.

"But when she could hide him no longer, she got a papyrus basket for him and coated it with tar and pitch. Then she placed the child in it and put it among the reeds along the bank of the Nile." Exodus 2:3 (NIV)

Don't Die In Your Nest

Is your life being stirred, shaken and interrupted? Have you rebuked the devil and he's not listening to you? I'll tell you why. The Lord has greater things for you. Like an eagle, He has landed and is shaking the hell out of the place where you're at. Embrace the shaking and kiss your normal life goodbye. It's time to spread your wings and fly, because you're an eagle, not a chicken. Don't die in your nest.

"As an eagle stirreth up her nest, fluttereth over her young, spreadeth abroad her wings, taketh them, beareth them on her wings." Deuteronomy 32:11 (KJV)

Welcome To the Real World of Ministry

Being misunderstood for many years drove me into the arms of Jesus. It was a blessing in disguise, for it shaped me more into His image and helped refine my prophetic gift.

When Jesus says, "Follow Me," somewhere in your journey you will be misunderstood. Be careful when all men speak well of you. If you've never been misunderstood, check your pulse.

"Blessed are those who are persecuted because of righteousness, for theirs is the kingdom of heaven. Blessed are you when people insult you, persecute you and falsely say all kinds of evil against you because of Me. Rejoice and be glad, because great is your reward in heaven, for in the same way they persecuted the prophets who were before you." Matthew 5:10-12 (NIV)

"There isn't
a demon
behind
every
locked door."

"Don't Go Pickin' a Fight with the Devil"

I will never forget these words the Lord spoke to me many years ago at the height of much spiritual warfare in my life. He said, "Son, don't go pickin' a fight with the devil. I totally defeated satan on the cross. If you think you need to fight satan one-on-one to defeat him, you will start believing that My victory wasn't enough. If you go looking for him, he will come looking for you."

Have you ever rebuked the enemy for several days and he wasn't listening to you? You found out later that God was in control of the situation the entire time. There have been times when I have rebuked the devil and I heard the Lord say, "It's not the devil, it's Me."

I have fought and lost some battles because they weren't my battles to fight, they were the Lord's. There isn't a demon behind every locked door; sometimes it's God's timing to keep the door closed a little while longer. The enemy's big trick is to make intercessors believe that if they are not fighting satan constantly they are not doing their job.

I believe we pay too much attention to the enemy and satan loves it! I regret that I wasted so many years fighting the devil when I could have been worshiping the Lord and exalting Him above all my enemies. There's a time and a place to take authority over him, but it's not 24/7 (24 hours a day, 7 days a week). Had I worshiped God more, I would have won more battles.

"Let God arise, let His enemies be scattered."
Psalm 68:1a (NAS)

Giants Are the Breakfast of Champions

I hear the Father asking, "How hungry are you? When you get hungry enough, you get to eat giants! The giants aren't showing up to take you out, they're showing up so you can eat them. Eat your giants today. They are your nourishment. They are your bread and sustenance. Giants are the breakfast of champions."

"Only rebel not ye against the Lord, neither fear ye the people of the land, for they are bread for us. Their defense is departed from them, and the Lord is with us. Fear them not." Numbers 14:9 (KJV)

"The world
won't stop
turning
if you take
a break."

Take A Break!

My wife and I went to Lancaster, Pennsylvania for a two-day getaway. At three in the morning, the title of this new book came to me. Many times, we need to get away to think straight and hear God's voice. The earth won't stop turning if you take a break. It was turning before you arrived here and it will keep turning after you're gone. Take a break!

"And He said to them, 'Come away by yourselves to a secluded place and rest a while.' (For there were many people coming and going, and they did not even have time to eat.)" Mark 6:31 (NASB)

God's Crazy Love Does It

In my worship time recently, I heard the Lord whisper, "I'm crazy about you, Bill. I'm absolutely crazy about you." I said, "What? Lord, why would You be crazy about me? I fall so short of Your glory." He said, "I know, but you trust Me. You still trust Me to do what you cannot do. That thrills Me. That's what makes Me crazy about you."

How about you? Do you know that you can thrill Him? Trust Him today and you will experience His crazy love for you and His peace that surpasses all understanding. The Lord would rather have us trust Him than figure Him out.

"What, then, shall we say in response to these things? If God is for us, who can be against us?" Romans 8:31 (NIV)

Section Two

Being Real With You

"I found myself
eating breakfast
before I realized
that I had
forgotten
to fast."

Amazing Grace Is When You Think You Have Blown It

For years I have chosen to fast every Thursday until supper. I fast for my family, ministry and for God to do what I can't do. This morning as I awoke, I was looking forward to fasting, but after taking a shower I found myself eating breakfast before I realized that I had forgotten to fast.

I felt grieved, for without fail the Lord always seemed to do something significant, especially in my ministry on my fasting day. I repented and knew that God would understand my forgetting, but I felt sure I would miss my blessing. I said, "Lord, I still trust you."

Late this afternoon, to my surprise, I received an email concerning an open door for my ministry. It surprised me, for I knew it didn't come through fasting. I then heard the Lord say, "Son, I just wanted you to know that it's in trusting Me, not in your fasting, that you receive My favor. In fact, because you felt grieved about missing your fast day, I counted this day as a three day fast on My calendar, with more blessings to follow. Have a nice day!"

"Moreover the law entered, that the offence might abound. But where sin abounded, grace did much more abound." Romans 5:20 (KJV)

"I have always been
self-conscious
about my
appearance
in photos or
on camera."

Do You Like How You Look?

I am struggling. A door has opened for me to be interviewed on television with my latest book. I have always been self-conscious about my appearance in photos or on camera because of the bump on my head that makes my eyes uneven. I wondered if this would take away from the interview. How could God get glory out of the way I look? I was close to canceling the invitation, but the Lord spoke to me, "Son, I could use you more if you looked worse." The scripture then came to me, *"My grace is sufficient for thee: for my strength is made perfect in weakness. Most gladly therefore will I rather glory in my infirmities, that the power of Christ may rest upon me."* 2 Corinthians 12:9 (KJV)

I never understood until now what a minister once said to me, "Bill, you have two things going for you. One is your humor and the other is the bump on your head. You get people's attention." I want to encourage you today. Whatever you think about your looks, God sees you differently. We are beautiful in His eyes and one day we'll all have perfect bodies in heaven, except for One. He will wear nail scarred hands throughout eternity. His name is Jesus. Oh, how I boast in His scars.

"Then he said to Thomas, 'Put your finger here; see my hands. Reach out your hand and put it into my side. Stop doubting and believe.' Thomas said to him, 'My Lord and my God.'" John 20:27, 28 (NIV)

"Here's the gold
that I have
found: 'Love's
gonna live
here again!'"

Despite The Mud On My Face, I Have Struck Gold!

I was given a prophetic word recently, that I was a spiritual prospector: one who digs in the earth looking for gold. In spite of all the dirt and mud, I have persevered and discovered the greatest treasures are hidden just beneath the gross, dark places of the earth. With mud on my face, I have struck gold!

Here's The Gold That I Have Found: "Love's Gonna Live Here Again!"

The largest deposit of gold the Lord helped me unearth is: "Love's gonna live here again!" This finding was so huge, I couldn't get over it, around it or underneath it to reveal it all. I could see that God's love will never reach our hearts until it blows our minds! It's a raging wild fire chasing us; a love that passes all knowledge. His unconditional love is beginning to invade the earth in this hour. Masses will be slain by it in a moment's time. Every person that's difficult for us to like, God's love is moving in on them. We're going to fall in love with people again, like we did when we first fell in love with Jesus.

God's love is going to invade us first and then the world. You may already be experiencing this. It happens on one of "those" days. Not a day when everything is going fine and you think you deserve God's love. He will wait you out until you have one of those days when all hell breaks loose, when you blow it big time and everything you do that day is wrong. You don't have a leg to stand on; you want to put a bag over your head and leave town. But, at that moment, He outruns you and stops you in your tracks and says, "I love you! I still love you! I don't love you because you are good or bad. I love you period. You can't earn My love. You can only receive it. You can't fail enough to stop Me from loving you."

When we get this, it will cause us to love Him back with all of our heart, mind, body and strength. "Returning to your first love" means to get back to allowing God to love you the way He did when He first found you. That's what changed you. That is what will keep you going strong the rest of your life.

One day I knew I fell short of the glory of God, but God still came and blessed me anyway. I said, "Lord, how can You put up with me and still love me?" He said, "Get used to it. It's easy. I loved you when I thought you up, before your mother's womb." Even when He disciplines us, it's out of His great love for us.

Don't Miss What God Is Doing Now

God is going to save people we wouldn't. He is going to use people we wouldn't. People who aren't even looking for Him, will be found by Him. Get used to this, it is now happening. *"I revealed myself to those who did not ask for me. I was found by those who did not seek me. To a nation that did not call on my name, I said, 'Here am I, here am I."* Isaiah 65:1 (NIV). People in your city who are not even looking for God, will be found by Him. As this happens, some of God's people will get upset thinking, "If I was God, I wouldn't save that person." That's why you are not Him. Get over it!

God's Love Keeps Blowing My Mind

I asked a state trooper recently, "How are things in your city?" He said, "It's sin city. If you knew what went on in this city, you wouldn't be able to sleep at night." I went home and was praying. I asked the Lord what He thought about this certain city. He said, "It's a great city. I love the people in it." I was waiting for Him to say more, but He didn't. I sensed the Lord saying, "If I did sleep at night, which I don't, it wouldn't be their sin that would keep Me awake. It would be My love grieving for them."

I Heard the Lord Say, "I'm Untying Donkeys Again!"

It's interesting that Jesus chose a donkey that was never tamed or ridden by man, to ride on into Jerusalem. Why didn't He choose a beautiful white stallion that had years of training and adorned with honor? I wonder how many of His own people were disappointed in the way He came on such a despised, stubborn animal. God still comes in unpopular ways to confound the wise. God's foolishness is wiser than man's intelligence. Sometimes His own people miss Him in how He shows up in cities and nations.

I wonder what thoughts ran through the donkey's mind that day. Perhaps it was, "Why me?" But as its creator sat upon its back, that donkey must have neighed, "Why not me?" I sensed the Lord saying, "Untie the donkeys and bring them to Me. I am going to ride into cities and nations of the world on untamed and untrained donkeys (people) once again."

"If anyone asks you, 'Why are you untying it?' say, 'The Lord needs it." Luke 19:31 (NIV)

More Gold - "Keep Dodging Bullets"

I recently had a vision that I was going through a battle of heavy warfare. I saw myself running through gunfire of the enemy. Heavy army tanks were pointed my way and going off. I kept running, knowing that if I stopped it would be all over for me. But as I kept running, I kept dodging bullets. I surprised myself. Oh, I took some hits, got some wounds, but for some unknown reason, I just wouldn't quit running and kept trusting the Lord to keep me. I knew there was a call on my life and it caused me to keep going no matter what. There was a cause for me to fight for, and there was no fear in this vision. I had no fear in me. Trusting the Lord gave me peace.

I sense I am to impart this vision into you this day. Not just me, but the grandstands and all of heaven are shouting to you, "Keep dodging bullets! Keep dodging bullets!" Don't let the wounds stop you. Keep dodging the bullets! Your wounds are temporary. As you keep going, the Lord will heal your wounds. While in this vision, I remembered some hits that I have taken in this war. It started early, on a bike wreck when I was five years old. I still wear a scar on my head today. At seven years old, I had a brain tumor that God healed at Mercy Hospital, in Pittsburgh, Pennsylvania. Now, it's gone! Fifteen years ago, there was a blood clot in the artery of my heart. Three days later, my heart stopped on the table.

I've had so many physical tests in recent years, saying I shouldn't be here. But just when the doctors think that there is something terribly wrong with me, their conclusion is, "There's nothing wrong with you! There's nothing wrong with you!" I want to impart this into you today also,

35

into your spirit, soul, mind and body. I don't care what people or life's situations are saying about you, even a bad medical report, and no matter what anyone is telling you. Even the enemy shouting that you are unworthy. Listen carefully, "There's nothing wrong with you! There's nothing wrong with you! Because of what the cross and God's love did for us, there's nothing wrong with us."

He made us worthy and by His stripes we are healed! Trust Him and keep dodging the bullets. (I am not saying that taking medicine or going to the doctor is wrong, but keep saying in your spirit what God's word says and your body will begin to come under His shadow.)

More Gold - We Are Now In A "But God" Season

Saul was a terrorist persecuting the church... "but God" changed his name to Paul. Jonah ran from the call of God... "but God" had a whale with Jonah's name on it. You may be going through hell... "but God" has been to hell before. You may be bound by drugs and alcohol... "but God" still delivers. Your dream may have died... "but God" still raises dead things.

You may be going through hell's fire...but here comes the gold in your life! Keep digging!

"And now these three remain: faith, hope and love. But the greatest of these is love." 1 Corinthians 13:13(NIV)

Did You Ever Get Mad At God?

Years ago, I was frustrated because the Lord didn't answer a certain prayer the way I thought He would. I confess, I was not only frustrated but I was mad at God all day. That night as I was about to go to sleep, the Lord began to speak to me very clearly concerning a church where I would be ministering the following Sunday. I was surprised He was speaking to me since I was upset with Him and I wasn't speaking to Him.

I said to the Lord, "Why are You talking to me like this, when You know I've been mad at You all day?" The Lord responded, "Son, you may be mad at Me, but I'm not mad at you. My love is different than yours. I love you whether you love Me or not. I love you no matter what!" I repented immediately, seeing myself the way He sees me and yet loves me. I'm learning that God loves us on our worst days. He is for us, not against us.

"It is of the Lord's mercies that we are not consumed, because His compassions fail not. They are new every morning; great is thy faithfulness." Lamentations 3:22, 23 (KJV)

Confessions of a Spirit-Led Writer

I must confess something. I try not to write, but I just can't help it. It's like something beyond my control reaches down inside of me and picks up my pen. Am I addicted or in bondage? I thought for sure I was, as I cried out to the Lord, recently. I said, "Lord, free me from this addiction to write. I can't stop it. I would write if no one ever read what I wrote."

He spoke, "Son, I know how hard it is for you to stop and I'll tell you why you can't. You're not the one who's addicted to writing, I AM. Since you're addicted to Me, and I have given you this gift, I must continue to write through you and many others with the pen of a ready writer. I was writing before time began, for I am the Word, and I will be writing on the hearts of men as long as the earth remains."

I then asked the Lord, "Can I write when I get to heaven?" He said, "Yep, there's a whole lot to write about up here."

If you have a gift to write, you may be experiencing this at times in your life.

"Blessed be the LORD my strength, which teacheth my hands to war, and my fingers to fight." Psalm 144:1 (KJV)

I Have Found the Secret to Healing In My Life

This has to be the Lord, because I battle worry when it comes to my health. But lately, I have discovered when I'm in a doctor's office, I find myself thinking about what the Lord has next for me to do for Him. This takes me out of the doctor's office and into my future. It's like I'm not here anymore in my present health problems. At that moment, I'm no longer living just for today, but for my God given future. As I move into my God given future, every cell in my body gets excited about what God has planned for me.

As I get excited about my future, I believe my body gets in line for it. As God shows me my future, it must mean I am going to be healthy enough to do what God is showing me. I then start thinking about a good doctor's report and it happens.

I am discovering that my health is getting better by thinking this way. It's the Lord renewing my mind. Of course, diet and exercise are helping too but I can't help to wonder how much of our lives are influenced by the way we think.

"Finally, brethren, whatsoever things are true, whatsoever things are honest, whatsoever things are just, whatsoever things are pure, whatsoever things are lovely, whatsoever things are of good report; if there be any virtue, and if there be any praise, 'think' on these things." Philippians 4:8 (KJV)

More Can Happen Over a Meal than In Huge Conferences

It seemed to begin at the table right after we had eaten. There came such freedom to share our ups and downs in life as well as in ministry. Even as we shared our discouraging times and even the bloopers we made in ministry, something began to take place...a joy unspeakable and full of glory began to descend upon us.

Such freedom to share our hearts and become real people to each other seemed to untie heavy yokes that had somehow wrapped around us through everyday life, and the mundane stuff that goes with ministry. This joy began to trickle down from on high, and amazingly, our "downs" became our "ups" as the joy of the Lord began falling like an avalanche. I sensed the Lord saying, "You have just entered into the highest place of fellowship with Me!"

"Every day they continued to meet together in the temple courts. They broke bread in their homes and ate together with glad and sincere hearts, praising God and enjoying the favor of all the people. And the Lord added ed to their number daily those who were being saved." Acts 2:46, 47 (NIV)

Confessions of an Earthly Father

As I was praying recently over my own past and present shortcomings as a father, my feelings of failure were divinely interrupted by a still, small voice that spoke volumes to my broken heart...God said, "Son, you have been focusing on your weaknesses that your children seemed to have inherited. Have you forgotten that they also inherit strengths that you were born again with? Stop thinking of all those generational curses the enemy has been filling your mind with, that I took to the cross. Start renewing your mind about your children, for they are now only destined to receive generational blessings—the seed and the seed's seed of the righteous is blessed because of My righteousness that I have given you!"

"The seed of the righteous shall be delivered." Proverbs 11:21b (KJV)

Your children's spiritual DNA - "DESTINY NOW ARISING!"

"You May Have Failed Your Children...But I Won't."

God says, "I'm turning the hearts of the fathers to their children. (See Malachi 4:6) This means I am taking what is good and pure and lovely and of good report from inside the hearts of the fathers, and I am pouring it into the hearts of their children. 'I am turning the hearts of the children to their fathers' means I am taking what is good and pure and lovely and of good report from inside the hearts of the children and pouring it into the hearts of their fathers. You and your children will experience overwhelming love that will overcome evil with good. Mothers will be caught in the crossfire of this love explosion as My love flows unhindered between the fathers and the children!"

"For whatsoever is born of God overcometh the world: and this is the victory that overcometh the world, even our faith." 1 John 5:4 (KJV)

"Faith Runs In Your Family!"

The Lord is also including mothers in this word. Paul told Timothy, *"When I call to remembrance the unfeigned faith that is in thee, which dwelt first in thy grandmother Lois, and thy mother Eunice; and I am persuaded that in thee also." (2 Timothy 1:5 KJV).* I believe Paul was reminding Timothy that "faith runs in your family!"

Faith is contagious and faith runs in YOUR family, too! I believe many of our children will end up in the "Hall of Faith," that continues to be written from the book of Hebrews in chapter eleven.

«...who through faith subdued kingdoms, wrought righteousness, obtained promises, stopped the mouths of lions. Quenched the violence of fire, escaped the edge of the sword, out of weakness were made strong, waxed valiant in fight, turned to flight the armies of the aliens..." Hebrews 11:33-34 (KJV)

Section Three

God Is Going for the Real in Us

I Cried Out To God,
"What Are You Doing To Me?"

I felt I could no longer endure the painful trial going on in my life for so long. In frustration, I cried out to God, "What are You doing to me?" He said, "I'm making a man of God out of you!" He continued, "I did not cause your pain, but I'm using it."

The orthopedic doctor calls it a frozen shoulder. Jesus calls it healed. It's a muscle beneath the shoulder that becomes locked up and is very painful. The orthopedic doctor said, "You must stretch your arm to loosen that muscle. Here are six exercises, twice a day for six weeks, including hanging on a bar. You must stretch your arm until it hurts. Then lean into the hurt and count for twenty seconds with excruciating pain and then repeat." After a few exercises, I thought about the doctor, "He's got to be kidding me! It feels like I'm tearing my muscle apart; like I'm ripping it out of my arm."

Is It A Good Pain or A Bad Pain?

He also advised me to visit a massage therapist. As she was working on my arm muscle, I had to let her know something. "It hurts! That's painful!" She asked me a question, "But is it a good pain or a bad pain?" I said, "I'm a no pain person."

I was told if you want to recover faster, you can have someone else stretch your arm because they will pull it farther than you would. I thought to myself, "How stupid is that?" But, in desperation to end this ordeal, I chose a physical therapist to stretch my arm. The pain was so great, I laughed. I said to him, "Am I going crazy? Why did I laugh when I felt the worse pain in my life?" He said, "That's your release! That laughter is your release!" I now believe pain can be an ingredient in laughter. I promise, if you are now in pain that is beyond words, there will be a time when you will laugh again, and even drown in God's laughter.

"Blessed are you who weep now, for you shall laugh." Luke 6:21b (ESV)

There was a time when my pain almost stopped this ministry. On one ministry trip I became so powerless to the pain that I justified not going to the next meeting. My wife prayed, but no relief. I phoned home to our intercessors for prayer. One intercessor, after praying said, "Bill, you are on a mission. God has sent you there. You can trust Him." Something clicked in my spirit. I dragged my whole body to that meeting. The moment I stood up to minister, the pain left me.

After the meeting, it returned with a vengeance. It fought me to the next meeting two days later. When I got up to minister, it left again and then followed me home. As this took place with many of my meetings, something dawned on me. I am stretching my spiritual muscles! I want to encourage you. Sometimes you must walk through some stuff to get to where God is. But remember, you are on a mission and the great I AM has sent you!

Spiritually Frozen Muscles in the Body of Christ

Many times, what I experience in my physical body, is what is going on in the body of Christ. I sense the Lord showing me that there are some spiritually frozen muscles in His body. And, I hear the Lord saying, "You need to stretch those muscles. Stretch them until it hurts! Many of your healings will come while you are being stretched by others. I am stretching you this season out of your frozenness. I am stretching your arms farther than you would like, so they can reach around a world full of pain, sin and brokenness. Those frozen muscles will thaw by the fire of My Spirit, if you allow Me to stretch you."

Being Stretched Against the Odds

"And it shall come to pass in that day, that his burden shall be taken away from off thy shoulder, and his yoke from off thy neck, and the yoke shall be destroyed because of the anointing." Isaiah 10:27 (KJV)

After several months of pain, prayers of many, stretching exercises and some laser treatment, my frozen shoulder is finally loosed. The pain is gone. God has intervened again in my life.

Lord, help us to keep stretching and allowing You to stretch us beyond the pain.

"For our light affliction, which is but for a moment, worketh for us a far more exceeding and eternal weight of glory." 2 Corinthians 4:17 (KJV)

A Titanic Move of God is Coming Out of the Deep, Troubled Waters

"And I will compensate you for the years the locusts have eaten-the larval locust, the hopper locust, and the fledging locust." Joel 2:25a (MEV)

Recently during worship, I began to see in the Spirit the movie, "Titanic", as though it was beginning to play backwards (in reverse). This movie started out at the very tragic end, where people had died and their bodies lay frozen on rafts in the ocean. But then, the ice on the frozen bodies and rafts began to melt. And then, the dead started breathing again and moving. I then saw this huge Titanic ship begin to slowly rise up out of the sea, with its tail rising upward as in slow motion.

I sensed the Lord saying, "I am restoring and resurrecting what has died and has been lost down through the generations of the great moves of My Spirit!"

I believe I saw what the next move of God through worship will look like.

'Titanic' Worship Is Coming!

The lifeless orchestra players on this rising Titanic began breathing new life again, and this time, it was as though heaven's angels were singing with the orchestra over the earth, land and sea. The songs now were not songs of goodbye or hoping to go to heaven through God's amazing grace, but these new songs were actually pulling on heaven, bringing heaven down to earth.

These new songs were songs with so much unspeakable joy and eternal life in them that the deceased people on the ship and the rafts danced out of their frozen watery graves, worshiping God in the highest. The sea was now giving up her dead.

A Change in Captains: "I Will Take Over From Here!"

All that was lost had been regained, and then some. This huge ship continued to float with a heavenly stability. The Titanic, as big as it once was, appeared to grow even larger. I then saw the captain of the ship and recognized him as resembling the Son of God. I heard Him shouting with love, "I will take over from here!" Immediately His voice echoed and was heard over many waters and lands. Lifeboats were being tossed overboard as far as the eye could see, as people from all nations, tribes and tongues were reaching to Him and crying out to be saved. Multitudes were now coming in out of their troubled waters.

This movie continued and seemed to end before the huge iceberg was hit which caused the catastrophic tragedy. Being a little concerned about what had crippled the ship, I asked the Lord, "What about the huge iceberg that brought this Titanic down?" I sensed the Lord saying, "Forget those things that are behind you and sail on!"

"In the last days, God says, I will pour out my Spirit on all people. Your sons and daughters will prophesy, your young men will see visions, your old men will dream dreams." Acts 2:17 (NIV)

48

"Don't miss

your

training

moment."

"I Am Using the Chaos in Your Life"

While walking to a park near our home recently, I heard loud shouting, like a crowd going wild, long before I arrived. As I approached the bottom of a field, I saw hundreds of men in black uniforms running to and fro as the shouting continued nonstop.

Officers were shouting commands in the faces of young men. At times the commands were to run across the field only to find another officer shouting back at them, "No, go back where you came from!" The whole scene was pandemonium.

I asked someone, "What is going on?" They said, "It's the Marines. They are drilling young men before they go to boot camp."

Later, as I was walking, I met two of the officers. I said, "What is all the constant shouting about? Some are losing their voices."

One of them said, "It's to create chaos so they learn how to function in the midst of it. On the battle field, when the guns are firing, they need to learn to shout loud enough so their comrades can hear them." This day would give these young men the final opportunity to change their minds about joining the Marines.

I then knew the Lord was speaking loud and clear to me and to the body of Christ. The chaos, that makes us feel like quitting and running away, actually becomes our training moment. It comes to train us to function in the midst of it. The God of the angel armies is teaching us to reign in a crazy world; to rule in the midst of our enemies. He's using the chaos in our lives, He's not wasting it.

"When thou goest out to battle against thine enemies, and seest horses, and chariots, and a people more than thou, be not afraid of them: for the Lord thy God is with thee, which brought thee up out of the land of Egypt." Deuteronomy 20:1 (KJV)

Don't Do It

There's something that has stayed with me throughout this day that I must share, even if it's for one person. I heard the Father say, "There are those who feel so forgotten and forsaken, that they are considering suicide. Tell them, 'Don't do it.' I am coming their way."

Your life is as dark as the inside of a tomb and you feel dead. Listen carefully, "Often before a miracle, there's dead silence. But Jesus is coming your way. Tell your tomb goodbye. The Lord has great plans for you."

"For when the spirit of death wrapped chains around me and terrifying torrents of destruction overwhelmed me, taking me to death's door, to doom's domain, I cried to you in my distress, the delivering God, and from your temple-throne you heard my troubled cry. My sobs came right into your heart and you turned your face to rescue me." Psalm 18:4-6 (The Passion Translation)

"God has
been in my
interruptions
more than
He's been
in my plans."

This Is The Moment You Were Born For and The King Is Calling For You!

I heard these words recently, "We gotta 'Go' for launching! We gotta 'Go' for launching!" Then it dawned on me. There can be no launching without a great shaking. I don't know about you, but I'm sitting at the edge of my seat for what's coming next, for the King is calling.

The King Calls for Us in Many Ways to Launch Us

"As an eagle stirreth up her nest, fluttereth over her young, spreadeth abroad her wings, taketh them, beareth them on her wings." Deuteronomy 32:11 (KJV)

Forty years ago when I started attending our church, in the Spirit, I saw a huge eagle in a nest in our balcony. It was stirring the nest in people's lives. It stirred and shook twenty-six of us members out into full-time ministry. Some went overseas and never came back, except for visits, for they fell in love with people over there. Some like myself stayed in the states. After forty years, I saw this eagle returning to our church and to the body of Christ at large. The eagle has landed! The eagle has landed in our lives!

The Eagle Has Landed To Stir Up Our Spiritual Gifts and Talents

When the eagle landed forty years ago in our church, it began to stir a hunger inside of me to hear God's voice. Back then, I lived two blocks up the street and I would walk to church begging God to let me hear His voice in the church service, for I needed to know what to do with my life. Because I was expecting to hear from the Lord Himself, He never failed to anoint my pastor or anyone else who stands in our pulpit to minister exactly what I needed to hear. For forty years in the same church, God still speaks to me, for my expectation is to hear from Him.

This eagle will stir, shake, and interrupt our lives. Looking back over my life, God had been in my interruptions more than He's been in my plans. I hear the Lord saying, "Kiss your normal life goodbye!" Your nest has had some nice comfortable feathers in it, but this year, as the nest shakes, the sharp sticks will jab and prick us out of our comfort to help us get out of the nest, because we were born to fly.

Every storm and adversity you have ever faced has come to prepare you to spread your wings this year. Don't die in the nest. The harvest is now. God often comes when we least expect it, when we are just going along in life minding our own business, and our dream is within reach and we're almost there. That's when the eagle often lands, interrupting our lives, to be about our Father's business.

The Lord says, "There'll be no sitting on the sidelines this year. I'm taking the benches out. There'll be no benches to sit on. I'm calling everyone onto the field of their neighbors, city sidewalks, market places and the nations. Wherever you go, I'll be there." The move is on! The King is calling for you.

"I Am Up To Something Good!"

"Prepare for take-off! Make sure your seat belts are fastened securely." These were the words my wife, Dagmar and I recently heard sitting on a plane to Houston, Texas, while waiting to take off. We were on our way to minister. Then the pilot came on the intercom and said, "We are expecting a nice flight to Houston today. I want to let you know, that I have more flying experience than Captain Sully, who landed the plane in the Hudson River." When I heard this, I said, "Thank you Lord, we are on the right plane with the right pilot." A little later he says, "I see a couple minor things up here that concern me. I will get the mechanics to check it out, then we'll be on our way." After a while he says, "I have good news for you and I have bad news. The good news is, you will be going to Houston. The bad news is, not on this plane." Those words pierced me and have never left me, for I believe it's a prophetic word for the body of Christ this season.

I heard the Lord say, "You will be arriving at your destination that I have for you this year, but not by sitting in the pews of your churches. These pews will not take you there, neither will this nest." We had to exit the plane to board another. Standing in a long line to board again, they announced yet another gate change for another flight. (There will be some gate changes coming for many of us this year.) I was frustrated with all these changes. I said, "Lord, what are you doing, because I'm on a mission for You?" He said, "First of all, I just saved you from a plane crash. Another thing, I'm up to something good!" Many of God's people with all the stirring, shaking and interruptions are wondering, what is going on in their lives. They are wondering where God is or where He went.

Let me tell you, God is up to something good in your life. He is reaching down and taking the good, the bad, and the ugly and stirring it all around and causing everything to work together for the good for them who love Him and are called according to His purpose. He has even pulled the stinger out of death and is using it for His glory.

From the Pit, to the Prison, to the Palace, the King is Calling for You

"Then Pharaoh sent and called Joseph, and they brought him hastily out of the dungeon; and he shaved himself, and changed his raiment, and came in unto Pharaoh." Genesis 41:14 (KJV)

There are many of you who feel like you've been in a pit for a long time. Others have felt like you've been in a prison, but we are in a "but God" season. This is the moment the King is calling you to the palace.

I think we have a wrong impression of what that palace was like for Joseph, being second in command. The Bible doesn't describe how beautiful that palace was, but it does talk a lot about the reason God brought him there. *"...but God meant it unto good, to bring to pass, as it is this day, to save much people alive."* Genesis 50:20 (KJV). Joseph considered the palace just a launching pad to launch his dream to save the people.

A king was building a palace in another country. He ordered huge pieces of glass mirrors to hang on the walls of the palace. When the shipment arrived, most of them were broken during the shipment. He became so angry that he said to his servants, "Break these huge pieces of glass into tiny pieces and throw them away." So, they began smashing those huge glass mirrors into pieces. As they were sweeping up all of the tiny pieces of glass to throw in the dumpster, one of the servants said to the king, "Oh king, this stuff looks like diamonds!" As the king looked down on all those broken pieces, he had a divine thought. He had his servants pick up all those tiny broken pieces and he began pasting them all over the walls of the palace. When people came and began admiring the diamonds filling the walls of the palace, the king would finally tell them, "What you are looking at is just tiny pieces of glass."

Though hidden, the broken and crushed in spirit will rise out of the dust and ashes of life. God is making diamonds out of the dust this year. He's making diamonds out of us. This is the year for broken people to be healed and redeemed. Our King will be decorating the walls of His palace house with broken people who shine like diamonds in His kingdom.

We're Not in Kansas Anymore!

Like Dorothy, we can't go back and live like we used to and do the things we used to do. We will have to think differently, for we are in a new place.

The King is calling for you and me. This is the moment we were born for. Ask the King what's next for you. Don't be surprised by what you hear. It may blow your mind.

"His (Jesus') mother said to the servants, "Do whatever he tells you." John 2:5 (NIV)

Stay Focused: Don't Compare Yourself to Anyone

I'll never forget watching the Olympics several years ago as Gabby Douglas, "the flying squirrel," won gold for best gymnastics. Instead of watching her opponents perform, she would bury her head in a towel to stay focused on her goal.

The Olympic swimmers wouldn't dare to glance at other swimmers in their racing lanes. A one second peek could cost them the gold.

Every person you compare yourself to, slows you down from reaching your dream. Remember, when you compare yourself to someone, there are ten people comparing themselves to you.

Stay focused and run your race to win.

"Because the Sovereign LORD helps me, I will not be disgraced. Therefore, I have set my face like a stone, determined to do His will. And I know that I will not be put to shame." Isaiah 50:7 (NLT)

"If your
family tree
is being shaken,
you are right on
schedule."

The King Is Calling for Your Family

If your family tree is being shaken, you are right on schedule. I see this eagle landing and shaking the hell out of many family trees right now. This shaking alone will bring in your spouse, children and grandchildren into God's kingdom, like nothing else has. It will bring orphans in out of the storm.

Many parents are wondering where and how to pass their baton onto the next generation. Don't be surprised that through this great shaking, you discover your baton falling down through the family tree and being caught by your children and grandchildren. Caution: they will most likely take your legacy and ministry in a whole new direction to reach a unique generation.

Can you hear the rustling of the leaves at the top of your family tree? Rejoice, God is beginning to blow His breath like a mighty wind into your family's nostrils to live again.

"Believe in the Lord Jesus, and you will be saved—you and your household." Acts 16:31 (NIV)

"Never
tell God
what you
don't need."

Talk About Freedom from Old Mindsets

I did it. For the first time in my life, I bought a smartphone, an iPhone 7 today. As I walked out of the Sprint door with it, I felt a chain snapping off my mind, breaking an old mindset of me thinking, "I don't need one." I then heard the Lord say to me, "Now here we go, let's spread the gospel further!"

Never tell God what you don't need.

"And be not conformed to this world; but be ye transformed by the renewing of your mind, that ye may prove what is that good, and acceptable, and perfect, will of God." Romans 12:2 (KJV)

"God keeps
changing
my mind
on things."

Talk About Money

After obeying the call of God, by leaving a good paying steel mill job with a sizable bank account, the Lord spoke to me, "I want to talk to you about My money in your bank account. Since I haven't given you someone to marry yet, you won't be needing it right now, but others do."

I secretly wrote out the largest check in my life. As I wrote the check, I felt like a saw was cutting on my shoulder blade. Many years of hard earned money was now escaping me through the tip of a pen. I have noticed that before the Lord can trust us with spiritual riches, He will challenge us with our wallets.

"So if you have not been trustworthy in handling worldly wealth, who will trust you with true riches?" Luke 26:11 (NIV)

It's Time for the Harp, Pen, Paintbrush and Dancing Shoes

"By the rivers of Babylon we sat and wept when we remembered Zion. There on the poplars we hung our harps, for there our captors asked us for songs, our tormentors demanded songs of joy; they said, 'Sing us one of the songs of Zion!' How can we sing the songs of the Lord while in a foreign land?" Psalm 137:1-4 (NIV)

When I first started traveling in ministry 20 years ago, I would sing in every meeting. One day, I stopped singing. I was in so many different churches with so many styles of music that the devil (and certain people) made me feel like my music didn't belong. So, I stopped. The passion laid dormant for many years, until recently. Within a week, two different people said to me, "Bill, when are you going to sing again?" I thought that was strange. I then heard God speak to me, "Son, it's not about the style of music— it's the anointing! Take your harp (your guitar and songs) down off the weeping willow tree and start killing the giants in people's lives."

Now, after fifteen long years, I have taken my harp (the call to sing) down off the weeping willow tree. God, through me, has come alive again! I don't know what I sound like to those listening, I just know that it sounds beautiful to God. He missed it for fifteen years.

Let me tell you a secret: we are not supposed to fit too tightly in the body of Christ when it comes to using our gifts and talents. God loves variety! That's why He never gets bored. Dare to be different if you want to see the glory of God in your life, city, and nation this year. Dare to obey the Lord with the unique gifts and ways He wants to use you.

Someone, Please Tear the Roof Off of God's House!

Do what God is calling you to do, regardless of what some people may think, and if need be, tear the roof off of God's house to let His glory in. Someone, please tear the roof off. Tearing a roof off can be risky. Many people will wonder why you are doing it. But we must see God's glory in our lives, cities, and the nations. Without God's glory, we perish. God has spoken and it is time for us to grab our harps, pens, paintbrushes, and dancing shoes and put them back into action again! God reserved this year for you! He is calling your name.

"And it came to pass, when the evil spirit from God was upon Saul, that David took an harp, and played with his hand: so Saul was refreshed, and was well, and the evil spirit departed from Him." 1 Samuel 16:23 (KJV)

Prison Bars Are Melting

I heard the Lord say, "I've found Me a people who have lost everything, with nothing left to lose. I will get great glory out of these, for they will have all of Me. I have hung the earth upon nothing and I will use nothing again for My glory."

"Turn you to the stronghold, you prisoners of hope; even today do I declare that I will render double to you." Zechariah 9:12 (KJV)

"Many have

been rejected

from My

own house!"

Rough Diamonds Are Getting God's Attention

I sense the Lord saying, "I'm releasing My glory through rough, unpolished diamonds in the earth...many have been rejected from My own house!

Many of these vessels, who seem more 'earthy' than others, will begin to shine even brighter as My glory pierces through their cracked and broken vessels. The defects in some earthen vessels will actually give way to more of My glory shining through them."

The most valuable fine cut diamonds in the world can only be seen in museums under lock and key and can never be touched by human hands. Diamonds in the "rough" can turn up anywhere and can be touched by anyone. Be careful who you think has a lot of earth left in them after they meet Jesus...there may be a larger diamond inside them!

"But we have this treasure in earthen vessels, that the excellency of the power may be of God, and not of us." 2 Corinthians 4:7 (KJV)

"Beware of
the enemy's
knock-out
punch."

Stay Out Of The Ring!

This is for many who the enemy is beating up on, with the statement, "You failed again. God is through with you." That is his knock-out punch. Many of God's saints have given up because they got in the boxing ring thinking they had to fight for their victory over sin, sickness and the devil. It was a fight that was never intended for them. Jesus totally defeated satan at the cross and handed us the victor's crown.

No wonder we are more than a conqueror through Christ because we weren't even in the ring when that happened. Now the enemy wants us to fight him and get in his ring to make us think we need to do something to earn God's grace and our victory. What a lying devil he is. The only fight the Lord tells us to do is, fight the good fight of faith. Just believe what Jesus has already done for us, period. It's a good fight, because He's already won it for us. So, stay out of the ring! The bell has rung. Your fight is over.

"But thanks be to God, which gives us the victory through our Lord Jesus Christ." 1 Corinthians 15:57 (KJV)

More than Conquerors

"What, then, shall we say in response to these things? If God is for us, who can be against us? He who did not spare his own Son, but gave him up for us all- how will he not also, along with him, graciously give us all things? Who will bring any charge against those whom God has chosen? It is God who justifies. Who then is the one who

condemns? No one. Christ Jesus who died- more than that, who was raised to life- is at the right hand of God and is also interceding for us. " Romans 8:31-34 (NIV

Many Are Coming In 'Out of Left Field' Into My Kingdom

While watching a recent baseball game, I noticed that a player, who had dropped a ball in a previous game, was playing poorly again. Feeling frustrated, I thought to myself, "Why doesn't the coach take that guy out of the game and replace him?" I sensed the Lord then say to me: "For the same reason I don't take you out of the game. The coach knows that guy is a better player than he appears to be right now." The next time that player stood up to bat, he hit a home run! It humbled me.

Don't count yourself or anyone else out of the game or God's Kingdom.

"For though the righteous fall seven times, they rise again, but the wicked stumble when calamity strikes." Proverbs 24:16 (NIV)

Section Four

Finding the Real in Others

"What
stormy seas
will he call
you to
walk on?"

Favored To Live

I faced my terror by night. It was afraid of me. And the arrow that flies by day; it missed me. You may wonder what my terror and arrow was. Just terror and an arrow, that's all it was (see Psalm 91:5).

Jesus' birth takes place at night (Silent Night, Holy Night). Then came a dark night in history filled with terror when King Herod ordered every two-year old boy and under to be killed (see Matthew 2). Satan dreads heaven coming to earth. But the Father whispers, "Can't touch him!" As believers, satan targets us also. If it's the darkest time in your life, be encouraged. Jesus is about to show up. I find Him in the darkest moments. That's when I've gotten to know Him, the power of His resurrection and the fellowship of His sufferings. Fear not, He will come and save you.

In a recent movie, the lead actress battled untold suffering and terror. The end was a bloody finish. Her youthful, battered body laid lifeless, turning the theatre into a morgue. After what seemed like eternity, her eyes popped open and she lived. I found out later that she was favored to live through her afflictions, so she could star in the next movie series. Looking back over my life, I can relate to this. Yes, I have survived everything so far and I am an overcomer. God has favored me to live through the hardest times. He has favored you, too. He has another series of our life to be lived. Our times are in His hands (see Psalm 31:15).

Walking On Giants

In Charlestown, South Carolina, a little boy, about four years old, walked over, looked up at me and said, "You are little!" I said to the pastor standing beside me, "What did he say?" The pastor said, "It sounds like he said, 'You are little!'" It made the boy feel good since he was so short, but it humbled me. It made me think. We should look at our biggest giant or mountain and say, "You are little!" It will humble any mountain or giant to fall. What mountain or giant will the Lord raise up for you to stand on top of this coming year? What stormy seas will He cause you to walk on?

On the Sea of Galilee, famous for storms, I asked the Lord a question. "Lord, are we near the place where Peter got out of the boat and walked on the raging sea before he fell?" The Lord answered me, "What do you mean Peter fell? This is the sea where Peter walked!" He didn't mention Peter falling. Peter sank, but he walked on water. I believe the eleven sat in the boat living in regret. The terror of that storm paralyzed them. They missed that once in a lifetime opportunity. Sinking is better than sitting. When life is over, we won't regret taking a risk for God and sinking. We will regret sitting. And God won't remember us sinking.

The Stage Is Being Set

When it looks like it's impossible for me to win, God is setting the stage for something greater. For many, the stage is set. The curtains have not yet been cracked open. God is still moving behind the scenes to place us front and center. That's why we haven't been heard from yet.

Isn't it the stories in the Bible of the people who looked like they would never make it, that build our faith the most? The Lord writes their heroic exploits, beginning with them knowing the agony of defeat, silent nights of terror, with trouble becoming their friend. It seemed there was no hope of ever fulfilling their purpose. Be encouraged. God is not through writing your story...

"Jesus did many other things as well. If every one of them were written down, I suppose that even the whole world would not have room for the books that would be written." John 21:25 (NIV)

"Build an Altar
and Call the
Family
Together
for Prayer."

As Families Began Praying Together, I Heard the Heart of America Begin to Beat Again

The answer for our nation may not be far from home. In the Spirit, as I began to hear families praying together, I sensed the Father saying, "I can hear the heart of America beginning to beat again, and I can feel its pulse!"

I sense the real warfare over our nation is against the very core of the nation: the family! I have heard many types of prayer alerts for our nation at this time, but I sense an urgent call from the throne room, for families to pray together at this critical time in our nation.

The Power of Prayer in Our Family

I believe we have overlooked and underestimated the power of prayer in our families. There is something about families that touches and moves the heart of God. Besides Adam and Eve, the Lord intended their family to subdue the earth to bring His kingdom into the affairs of this world. I believe satan feared the seed of the woman - for it would have the power to destroy him, for our children shall contend with their enemies in the gate (see Psalm 127:5) and *"Your descendants will take possession of the cities of their enemies."* Genesis 22:17 (NIV)

Before you think that it would be impossible for you to get your whole family to pray together, let alone to just be together, let me remind you of what the Bible says, "… *if two of you shall agree on earth as touching anything, … it shall be done"* Matthew 18:19 (KJV), or *"one (man) chase a thousand, and two put ten thousand to flight."* Deuteronomy 32:30 (KJV)

"God hath dealt to every man the measure of faith." Romans 12:3 (KJV). Since God has given "every man" a measure of faith, it is already in your family's DNA. As a believer (even if you are the only believer in your household), you can activate the faith in your family. Step out by faith and ask them to pray with you and see what happens! I believe your family will feel honored that you asked them and that you actually believe they are capable of praying. Watch what the Holy Spirit does, as those in your household even think about praying. I have seen the Holy Spirit hover over unbelievers as I have asked them to pray for me, and God has answered their prayer to prove Himself real. Perhaps, we have gone outside the family for prayer too often, when the Lord wants to work inside of our families to answer more of our prayers.

My House Will Serve The Lord!

There was a decree that turned the nation of Israel back to God, *"...as for me and my house, we will serve the Lord." (Joshua 24:15 KJV).* I believe, as Joshua was declaring to the nation of Israel to choose life or death, he was proclaiming the importance of not only his personal choice, but also his heart for his family. I sensed Joshua's heart for every father and mother was for them to decree that their families would serve the Lord, also. Was he sensing the power that families hold in influencing the whole nation from being destroyed? He believed if God could save his family, He could also save the whole nation.

Acts 16:31(KJV) says, *"Believe on the Lord Jesus Christ, and thou shalt be saved, and thy house."* I sense that we need to decree now more than ever that our whole household shall be saved and begin to decree over America, "One Nation under God!" Our Father still has this dream in His heart that not only your family but a whole nation can be saved—even in a day.

"Who hath heard such a thing? Who hath seen such things? Shall the earth be made to bring forth in one day? Or, shall a nation be born at once? For as soon as Zion travailed, she brought forth her children." Isaiah 66:8 (KJV)

Could it be, since the Garden of Eden, that the enemy well knows that families hold the hidden power to destroy his kingdom and deliver whole nations? Is it any wonder why he unleashes hell upon families?

Build an Altar and Call the Family Together For Prayer

I know many of you have been praying for your family, also. Yet, I am sensing an urgent call, as parents, not only to pray for our children, but to build an altar and call the family members together to pray with them. I sense our sons and daughters hold the keys to some of our own break-throughs and that we, as parents, hold some keys to our sons and daughter's healings and miracles that are needed as well. I believe there will now be a power released as we gather together as families to pray. Again, we cannot force our families to pray together, but even if one family member prays with us, I believe hidden power will be released in our lives, cities, and nation—perhaps the earth!

The Family That Prays Together Stays Together and has the Staying Power to Undergird a Nation!

Let's decree together, "As for me, my house and my nation, we will serve the Lord!"

Watch For Exit Signs to Light Up in This Season

I sense the Lord saying to many of us in transition, "Watch for the exit signs this season along major highways." This could mean a significant change of direction or a minor adjustment in our lives and ministry. Major highways speed up our traveling, but exits take us to our destination. Could it be that the Lord is calling many of us off the steering wheels of our ministry to get our hands on the harvest?

The Next Great Move of God Will Be Off the Beaten Path of Ministry

Why are so many people hearing a Lion roar at this time? When the Lion of Judah roars, His call is not tame. I believe He is roaring many of His people off the beaten path of ministry to forge their own trail to reach a chaotic world. These so called "crazy" ones will be accused of going too far to reach the lost, too far into the darkness to be the light, and have too many friends that are sinners. This is all because of God's compelling love. Aren't you thankful that He went too far for you?

There's a Time to Exit

I saw many of God's people driving down a major highway as their life and ministry were seemingly going wonderful. All of the sudden, I heard the Lord say to them, "Take the exit!" They appeared shocked, for they were certain they were well on their way to fulfill their God-given calling. Doubts and questions flooded their minds until the Lord spoke straight into their unaware fainting lives. "There's power off the next exit." Hearts began turning steering wheels, as a strong witness surged through their weary souls, confirming that it was God's voice. They hadn't noticed their gas gauge was resting on empty.

I will never forget what a young adventurous entrepreneur said to me three weeks into his God-given passion, "We already know the day will come when we will exit this ministry. It will become so successful and in demand that it will be real easy to pass it on to someone else so we can create and grow something new unlike the world has ever seen to touch millions." I was astounded at this young man's faith. I have never heard such faith spoken in ministry. To date, their ministry is like a wildfire blazing earth, without my divine wisdom. To exit means success to this young man, not failure. He plans on that day and looks forward to it. He told me, "As sure as there's a time to start, there's a time to exit."

We have a tendency to think the word exit represents something less when getting off a major road or ministry. But, it's actually God's way of promoting us into something more important on His calendar. It's not the end of the road; it's the bend in the road. Study the routes taken by God's chosen vessels and you will find exits in their callings.

A Barnyard Harvest

The byways tend to be places we are not familiar with, like barnyards. Recently, I heard the Lord say, "I'm releasing a 'barnyard anointing' to bring in the harvest. A barn and the harvest go together."

You gotta love a barn, if you want to see a harvest. You gotta love people, who act like animals, if you want a harvest. You gotta love horses because we, as His bride, are going to ride some wild horses. It's time to get back on the broncos and bulls that threw us off. We better love donkeys (people we thought the Lord would never use), because the Lord is untying them again to ride upon into cities and the nations of the earth.

Get used to the smell of barnyard manure if you want to reap a harvest. The number one spiritual fertilizer that helps us and everything else grow, is manure. It's harvest perfume. It's the perfume of harvest. Turn to someone near you and tell them, "I got a whole lot of fertilizer around me and something good is about to happen!" Don't be afraid to get your hands dirty in the harvest fields. The "barnyard anointing" will get your hands dirty.

"All Hands on Deck"

Recently I had a word for the Body of Christ, "All hands on deck." Now is the time to get our hands dirty. I saw the hand of the Lord reaching down and scraping the bottom of the barrel. The bottom was filthy and slimy. That's where He focused on reaching. I don't know about you, but He got His hands dirty when He reached way down for me. I was lost and undone without God and His Son reaching way down for me. Remember where He found us and where He is now finding others.

The Lord is coming to set our harvest fields on fire. The fire of God will be seen in your own backyard and afar off. We will discover the true fire is in the harvest. We will catch on fire as souls get born again. It's the fire in the harvest fields that will ignite our churches again. It's in the harvest fields where we will get our power back, for we will find nourishment and sustenance there. Jesus told His disciples when they brought food back to Him, when He was ministering to the woman at the well, He said, "I have meat that you don't know about."

I believe He wants to take many of us off of some main roads into the byways. Watch for those exit signs that will take us there.

"Then the master told his servant, 'Go out to the roads and country lanes and compel them to come in, so that my house will be full.'" Luke 14:23 (NIV)

Are You A Trail Blazer?

A minister for the states was communicating with a tribal leader, who had a village far out in the bushes, in a foreign country. The minister said to the tribal leader, "If you can tell me the road to get to where your village is, I will come and minister." The tribal leader responded back to the minister, "You better stay home. If you can't blaze a trail to get to where we are, you won't do us much good when you get here." The Lord is looking for trailblazers. Unless we have enough of God's love in us to compel us to blaze a trail and make a way where there is no way to reach the lost, we better stay home.

"As for us, we have all of these great witnesses who encircle us like clouds, each affirming faith's reality. So, we must let go of every wound that has pierced us and the sin we so easily fall into. Then we will be able to run life's marathon race with passion and determination, for the path has been already marked out before us. We look away from the natural realm and we fasten our gaze onto Jesus who birthed within us and who leads us forward into faith's perfection. His example is this; because his heart was focused on the joy of knowing that you would be his, he endured the agony of the cross and conquered its humiliation, and now sits at the right hand of the throne of God!" Hebrews 12:1-2 (The Passion Translation)

"Overlooked

Intercessors

Are Now

Needed For

Breakthrough!"

Calling In Our Kingdom Reserves

The meaning of reserve is: *"a fighting force kept uncommitted until strategic need arises-often used in the plural; a part of a country's armed forces not on active duty but subject to call in an emergency."* Merriam-Webster's Dictionary © 2017

"He that dashes in pieces is come up before thy face; keep the munition, watch the way, make thy loins strong, fortify thy power mightily!" Nahum 2:1 (KJV)

The heavens are rumbling. Angels scramble urgently as their assignments are shouted out, "Alert My people to call in their kingdom reserves! Walls of prayer protection have been breached, hindering the advancement of My kingdom! They must call in their reserves of 'intercessors' whom they have overlooked in the past but are urgently needed now."

Overlooked Intercessors Are Now Needed For Breakthrough!

Strong orders are being given to the saints, "Forgive every brother or sister who has wounded you. Be reconciled. Some were born to intercede for your life and ministry!" Brothers and sisters holding offense against one another are hindering physical healing and spiritual advancement. Some, whom they are refusing to forgive, have the gift of healing for their bodies.

Overlooked Family Members Are Waiting In Reserve to Receive Their Call for Duty

Overlooked family members, including children, grandchildren, and the unsaved, will launch many of God's people into never-before-seen breakthroughs.

I know myself and others have humbled ourselves before unsaved loved ones by asking them to pray for us. This knocked the walls down between the saved and unsaved. Many have experienced seeing unsaved loved ones pray themselves into God's kingdom through this kind of prayer request.

Many Children Need To Phone Home to their Parents to Call in Their Reserve of Wisdom to Win Their War

The older I get the more I realize my parents were right. When my mother was still living at ninety years old, there was seldom a day went by that I didn't call her on the phone. Why? I was still learning much from her. I think that's why God kept her living, for my sake and others. She kept outliving her doctors and diseases. Her wisdom was outlasting her enemies, and mine, too.

If Married, Your Spouse Is Your Most Powerful Intercessor Waiting In Reserve

I have many intercessors around the world praying for me and my ministry. One day, God showed me prayers from intercessors rising to the throne on my behalf. Then, all of the sudden, I saw my wife's prayer shooting upward like lightning, surpassing every other prayer on earth, reaching the Father's throne room instantly and getting immediate attention!

Don't ask your wife to pray "for" you, but to pray "with" you. Agreement in prayer produces victories that can take place in no other way! Praying in the Spirit together especially gives you an intimacy that brings breakthroughs in the natural realm.

The Name Of Jesus Is Waiting In Reserve To Shatter Your Enemy to Pieces!

I sense many are overlooking the power that is in the Name of Jesus, the name above every other name! Use it continually. When you just can't seem to pray…whisper the name of Jesus. The most powerful prayers in crises are the shortest. Just saying "Jesus" captures His attention and wreaks havoc in hell.

The Reserved Call for Ministries to Connect, Pray, and Flow Together In Battle

Has the Lord called you to ministry and then seemingly left planet earth? Does it seem like He is not paying attention to you and "your" individual ministry? The reason the Lord is not paying attention to "individual" ministries right now is because it isn't the season for individual ministries. God is seeing through corporate vision. He has the whole world in His heart. The best thing we can do is forget about ourselves and "our" ministry long enough to humble ourselves and prefer and esteem other's ministries above our own. Then reach out and connect with them to receive the corporate anointing He is releasing in this hour.

Each of us need corporate power to be launched into our purpose. As ministries confess their weaknesses and pray one for another, healing will flow like mighty waterfalls.

"Pull out all the stops and call in your reserves today… we are at war!"

"And from the days of John the Baptist until now the kingdom of heaven suffereth violence, and the violent take it by force." Matthew 11:12 (KJV)

An Earthly Father's Blessing

I sense many of you have been raised with an earthly father who loved you, but somehow failed to communicate his love and affirmation to you. You have grown up, but there is still an unanswered cry coming up out of you... "Daddy, where are you?"

Being an earthly father of three children and a man of God through the blood of Christ, I would like to pray right now over you to release an "earthly father's blessing" upon your life. By faith, I am going to stand in proxy (in the place of your earthly father), and lay my hand upon your head and speak an earthly father's blessing. Listen carefully, for many of you have never heard these words before, "I love you! I love you! You are so special. You were born to shake the world and there is nothing you cannot do! I am so proud of you! You are my beloved son, in whom I am well pleased! You are my daughter...you are daddy's favorite little girl in all the world! I love you! I bless you coming in and going out. I bless you in the market place, in the city, and in the field. I bless your wallets and purses that they will never know what lack is! I bless the fruit of your loins and your children's children."

In Jesus' Name, I break the generational curse of an orphan spirit off of you and your family. That orphan spirit that tells you, you don't belong. I bless those yet to be born, that they will be born crying, "My daddy loves me!" I cancel every negative curse word ever spoken against you in Jesus' Name. I bless you with an earthly father's blessing that cancels those curses.

As the Father has sent me, so I send you into your purpose and destiny. And nothing will stop you now. You will go the distance to finish what God has called you to do. I bless you and I love you...I love you...I love you! I bless you with an earthly father's blessing!

Father, open the heavens over these loved ones and show them how much You love them.

Tell someone, "My daddy loves me!"

"And a voice said, 'This is My beloved Son, in whom I am well pleased!" Matthew 3:17 (Berean Study Bible)

Be Patient - I Am Performing Major Heart Surgery on Your Nation

I heard the Lord say, "Be patient, your nation is having major heart surgery. Stay in the waiting room and pray."

I remember when my mother had major bypass surgery in her seventies. The doctors came to us in the waiting area and told us these words, "Because of what she just went through, she's not going to look very good to you, but she looks great to us!"

I sense the Lord saying, "Be patient with your nation, and remember I am not a Republican or Democrat, I AM that I AM. I AM working on a whole nation and everyone is a work in process. Don't judge, for I AM not finished working on anyone. I am working in the Fox News room, CNN News Room and all the other news networks and radio, TV outlets and media. I'm going for the heart of this nation or it will surely die, unless I complete surgery on its heart."

"Stop grumbling and complaining. It can delay and even cancel this kairos moment as your nation is on My operating table. Speak life and become love to every person. Embrace your opposition and enemies so they will experience My arms of love surrounding them. Protest the devil, not people."

"What appears to be chaos and gross darkness to you are instruments I pick up in My hands and use to give new hearts to nations. Nothing is being wasted in the hands of your Redeemer. Your heart is also included in this surgery. Trust Me, and tell your heart to beat again!"

"I urge, then, first of all, that petitions, prayers, intercession and thanksgiving be made for all people- for kings and all those in authority, that we may live peacefully and quiet lives in all godliness and holiness. This is good, and pleases God our Savior, who wants all people to be saved and to come to a knowledge of the truth." 1 Timothy 2:1-4 (NIV)

God Still Delivers

Many years ago at a Russ Bixler miracle meeting in Pittsburgh, Pennsylvania, I stood in proxy (stood in the place of) for my father, who for twenty-five years couldn't stop smoking cigarettes. When I arrived home, my father was in the living room watching television. I whispered to my mother in the kitchen, what I had done for dad so he would stop smoking.

I didn't know he overheard me telling mom. He walked into our kitchen and said, "Maybe that's the reason when I lit up a cigarette about eight o'clock this evening, it didn't taste right so I put it out." Dad never smoked another cigarette the rest of his life! It was the same time I stood in proxy for him that evening.

The Faith of the Centurion

"When Jesus had entered Capernaum, a centurion came to him, asking for help. 'Lord', he said, 'my servant lies at home paralyzed, suffering terribly.' Jesus said to him, 'Shall I come and heal him?' The centurion replied, 'Lord, I do not deserve to have you come under my roof. But just say the word, and my servant will be healed. For I myself am a man under authority, with soldiers under me. I tell this one, 'Go', and he goes; and that one, 'Come', and he comes. I say to my servant, 'Do this', and he does it.' When Jesus heard this, he was amazed and said to those following him, 'Truly, I tell you, I have not found anyone in Israel with such great faith.' Then Jesus said to the centurion, 'Go! Let it be done just as you believed

it would.' And his servant was healed at that moment."
Matthew 8:5-10 & 13 (NIV)

Section Five

Honest Nutrients

Short Words: Honest Nutrients

If you are believing for healing or a miracle, be careful who you hang out with. You better find three or four crazy people who believe, "All things are possible!"

God's not counting the times you fall down, He's counting the times you get back up. Get back up!

We fall down and we get up. Like doing push-ups, we get stronger.

For days I have been hearing these words in my spirit, "Sing your song, then get off the stage! Don't steal My show. Be careful what I'm anointing in your life doesn't take you off on a rabbit's trail."

I have discovered when you feel like quitting is when the Lord is using you greatly. No wonder the devil is telling you to quit.

I believe the greatest testimony we have that makes the devil tremble the most is, "I'm still here!" The enemy thought you quit. Boy, is he in for a big surprise.

Unless you're betrayed or rejected, you're not maturing in Christ. Your enemies have come to train you. Don't run! You may need a Judas like Jesus did, to launch you into your destiny.

Don't be afraid to be different from others. I think the difference is where the power is.

I am learning that when I feel intimidated by the enemy, that's when he is terrified of me. We are his enemy.

The Lord anoints people we wouldn't. He uses people

we wouldn't. He even saves people we wouldn't, without asking what we think. He acts like He's God.

I've noticed when the floods come, enemies rescue one another from drowning. There's revival in troubled waters.

Sometimes our worst is God's best, when He gets through with it.

David overcame his biggest giant called "criticism," right before he slew his smaller giant "Goliath."

All hell is breaking loose and all of heaven is breaking loose. But heaven is greater than hell.

"The Lord is
renaming
you today. Your
new name is
'Confidence!'"

"I'm Uprooting Insecurity and Fear in My People"

"...without being frightened in any way by those who oppose you. This is a sign to them that they will be destroyed, but that you will be saved-and that by God." Philippians 1:28 (NIV)

I have found a key that unlocks the cage of the Lion, who lives inside of us, as believers.

"Wherefore seeing we also are compassed about with so great a cloud of witnesses, let us lay aside every weight, and the sin which doth so easily beset us, and let us run with patience the race that is set before us." Hebrews 12:1 (KJV)

"Laying aside" is a powerful command that changes our perspective. When you lay something aside it is still there, but you don't focus on it, for the next verse says, *"Looking unto Jesus the author and finisher of our faith."* Now when intimidation attacks me, I have learned to lay it aside and do what God has called me to do.

The devil works overtime to steal our confidence to do the work of the Lord. But, we are not alone. The Lord allows our insecurities and fears to be exposed to deal with the root of them. So, be encouraged and don't stop. When you feel insecure or fearful, lay it aside and get up and let the Lion roar. God is faithful. *"Faithful is he that calleth you, who also will do it."* I Thessalonians 5:24 (KJV)

I received an email recently from a dear sister who plays piano for masses. She was fighting insecurity about performing perfectly at a special upcoming ceremony. I sensed the Lord giving me this word for her, "Lay aside your fear. Jesus will play the piano." Hours later, she sent me this response, "PRAISE REPORT! I just finished a run through the music and Jesus did indeed play the piano! I had to keep reminding myself that He was doing it and I didn't need to stick my nose in. When I first saw my friend Rachel, she asked me if I was ready. Very unlike, me, I answered 'Yes!' Praise the Lord!"

The Root of All Fears

Most of our insecurities and fears are surface symptoms with a deep root. The Lord deals with our weaknesses to make us strong. I have battled insecurity and fear most of my life. It started the moment my head hit the road so hard that it caused a bone growth on my forehead. The bike wreck happened when I was five. The trauma of what followed with surgery and doctor check-ups for most of my younger years, opened the door to a giant fear. A door that never got shut until recently.

I spoke at a conference recently in Gettysburg, Pennsylvania. I was checking out hotel prices. They were so high I wouldn't have been able to sleep at night. I kept looking around for a reasonably priced one. I found it; "The Cemetery Inn" near the battlefields. Arriving home after that weekend, greeting my wife, she said, "So and so called and he wants you to call him about those two cemetery plots he offered you a long time ago." I couldn't help but think; I just came from The Cemetery Inn and now someone is offering me two cemetery plots at half price. The half price concerned me too. I said, "Lord, I don't like the timing of this. I just came from ministering for You all weekend. What is going on?" Two days later I was to meet the brother at the cemetery memorial park to sign the transfer papers. After I arrived, I got tired of waiting in the office for him, so I went outside.

When I walked outside, all I could see were grave markers. As an eerie feeling came over me, the Lord spoke, "Son, this is the root of all your fears your whole life. Every doctor visit and the fear of every report of your physical exams have revealed - you are afraid to die. You battled it since the moment your head hit the road when you were five years old. When you were seven with a brain tumor, death hounded you again. Then, fourteen years ago, with a blood clot in the artery of your heart, with a fifty-fifty chance of survival, it stampeded you. Three days later with a heart catheterization, your heart stopped on that table and they jumped it back to beat again. Have you noticed by now I have never let you die? I still hold the keys to hell, death and the grave."

He continued, "What do you think about the scripture that says, 'To be absent from the body is to be present with Me?' No pain, no doctors, no devil. Fully alive in My unspeakable presence forever and ever? What are your thoughts on this?" For a moment, I was speechless. He was right. I just faced my worst fear that had made me vulnerable to an endless list of others. And, I failed to compare it to eternity. That day, I found peace in a cemetery. As I left those grave markers, He spoke again, "By the way son, the same power that raised Jesus from the grave lives in you. Go live. Go live. Don't be afraid of living. Enjoy every minute of it."

What's your fear? Fear of losing a loved one, a job, or your reputation? Maybe you are afraid to die and afraid to live. Drag your fears to Jesus today. Let His peace envelope you and His perfect love cast out all fear. Tell Him you are in this for the long haul no matter what.

"For God hath not given us the spirit of fear; but of power, and of love, and of a sound mind." 2 Timothy 1:7 (KJV)

Be Real and Be Healed!

I dedicate this book to all who struggle in their brokenness, imperfections and the sin that keeps nipping at our heels.

John Newton, author of Amazing Grace stated, "Although my memory's fading, I remember two things very clearly: I am a great sinner and Christ is a great Savior." (tags: biographical, inspirational)

The Bible answers our helpless condition: *"Turn your lives back to God and put your trust in the hope-filled gospel!"* Mark 1:15 (TPT)

"If we confess our sins he (God) is faithful and just to forgive us our sins and to cleanse us from all unrighteousness." 1 John 1:9 (KJV)

Our brokenness and imperfections actually attract Jesus to us. That's why He came. *"The Spirit of the Lord is upon me, because he hath anointed me to preach the gospel to the poor. He hath sent me to heal the brokenhearted, to preach deliverance to the captives, and recovering of sight to the blind, to set at liberty them that are bruised."* Luke 4:18 (KJV). That includes all of us.

Once forgiven, our past can often return to haunt us, causing emotional chaos and effecting our well-being. I believe the Lord is also handing us a key that's been lost for much needed healing in our lives: it's humbling ourselves before one another. *"Confess your faults (weaknesses) one to another, and pray one for another, that ye may be healed."* James 5:16 (KJV). I believe these four scriptures are the pillars of this book and are saying to us today: "Be real with God and be real with one another. Be real and be healed!"

Be encouraged as you listen to this song, *Our Sin & Guilt Erased,* and remember what Jesus has done for us:

https://www.youtube.com/watch?v=Wc0QPBslZoA

Words and Music by Bill Davidson © Bill Davidson, 2017, 1Purpose Music.

Bill Davidson
1Purpose Missions & Ministries
207 Sunnyside E.
Queensbury, NY 12804
Alliance International Ministries (aimteam.org)

Contact the Author

Bill Yount
Blowing the Shofar Ministries
132 E. North Ave.
Hagerstown, MD 21740
E-mail: theshofarhasblown@juno.com
www.billyount.com

If you would like to be blessed by the ministry of Bill Yount, please contact him at the above e-mail address. He is available to minister at your church, conference, meeting, coffee house or anyplace God's people are gathered in His Name.

Other books by Bill Yount are available at Amazon.com:

Some Hear Thunder... I Hear A Roar! / Supernatural Encounters & Stories to Encourage Your Heart

I Heard Heaven Proclaim / Prophetic Words of Encouragement

Prophetic Stones of Remembrance / A Legacy for the End Times